Backyard

Chicken

-The Practical Handbook on How to Raise a Healthy Flock-

By John Edwards

The information herein is offered for informational purposes solely and is universal as so. The presentation of the information is without a contract or any type of guarantee assurance.

The trademarks that are used are without any consent, and the publication of the trademark is without permission or backing by the trademark owner. All trademarks and brands within this book are for clarifying purposes only and are owned by the owners themselves, not affiliated with this document.

DISCLAIMER

All Erudition contained in this book is given for informational and educational purposes only. The author is not in any way accountable for any results or outcomes that emanate from using this material. Constructive attempts have been made to provide information that is both accurate and effective, but the author is not bound for the accuracy or use/misuse of information.

Table of Contents

5

CHAPTER ONE

Why Raising Chickens

Raising laying hens, as well as chickens, ducks, with poultry feed with the aim of eating quality meat and eggs produced directly in our courtyards is a stimulating activity that allows us to bring healthy products to our tables in the name of taste and naturalness.

Raising laying hens is easy and rewarding, however it is important to follow good breeding rules and guarantee the animals a correct diet to ensure maximum wellness and obtain an excellent result in terms of production.

You don't need to know everything to get results with your laying hen farm. A couple of laying hens will be enough for you to eat fresh eggs. Of course, you can also buy eggs at the supermarket with a specific expiration date but ... you won't have the same guarantees as you have from eggs just laid by hens! If you are afraid that raising laying hens is difficult, don't worry, it's very simple! You just need a little patience to get the hens used to laying eggs in the same place inside the chicken coop that you can build yourself or buy directly ready-made in specialized stores.

What is the Difference Between Hen, Chicken and Rooster?

It is a question that, sooner or later, many ask, but to which few can give a truly certain and precise answer, even though the hen is such an apparently familiar animal that we all believe we know well.

The difference between hen, rooster, chicken, chick, pullet, hen and capon is essentially based on two precise characteristics of the animal, age and sex, and on the basis of these that the initial question can find its certain answers.

It is clearly not an ontological and significantly existential question like the famous "Which came first, the chicken or the egg?", but it is still a very intriguing question, to which it is good to be able to provide the right answer, both for personal culture and above all because it will be very useful when you want to buy poultry specimens.

So, let's first see what a hen is and what are its physical and behavioral features.

HEN: SPECIES, NUTRITION, LIFE EXPECTANCY AND BEHAVIOR

The hen (species: gallus gallus; subspecies: gallus gallus domesticus) is a domestic bird of oriental origin raised by man for millennia for different purposes (eggs, food, companionship, ornament, etc.).

Chickens are interesting animals, as intelligent as mammals, such as dogs, cats and even primates. They are very sociable and enjoy spending time together, scratching for food, cleaning their feathers in dust baths, perching in trees and lying in the sun.

Chickens are precocious animals. The hens communicate with the unborn chicks, which respond by chirping from inside the egg!

Chicken is an omnivorous creature which, when living freely, loves to scratch the ground in search of seeds, grasses, earthworms and insects. The hen also usually swallows small pebbles that help her "shredding stomach" to separate and process the food better. The hen cannot make long flights anymore (at most a few tens of meters) and it can even lay 300 eggs in a year, depending on the breeds and live up to about 10/12 years (the longest-lived hen, Matilda, seems to have lived sixteen years).

It is a social animal that, in a group, is placed on the basis of a very precise "pecking order". Each chicken knows its place in this social scale and remembers the faces and the "degree" of over one hundred fellows, a social hierarchy that must be reconstituted when old chickens die or new members enter the group.

The classic sound of a hen is "clucking", but it is certainly not the only one; for every situation there is a precise noise.

The main characteristic of the hen is its ability to lay eggs; if inside the hen house there is also a rooster in fertile age, then, most likely, the eggs will also be fertile and, if hatched by the hen, will give birth to beautiful chicks.

DIFFERENCES BETWEEN HEN, CHICKEN, ROOSTER AND CAPON?

Here are all the various correct names to indicate poultry based on the age and sex of the specimen (considering that, usually, their lifespan is between 5 and 11 years).

Chick

Also known as a peep, this is a newly hatched chicken and in general of domestic fowl, covered with down (which will gradually replace the feathers); it feeds alone, guided or not by the hen.

Chicken And Pullet

Male and female (often chickens and pullets get confused because it is difficult to determine the gender). From about 41 days to reproductive age (they have not reached sexual maturity yet). They usually weigh up to 3.3 lb. The term derives from the Latin "pullastrum-am" from "pullus" with a termination indicating inferiority.

Hen

A mature female chicken, usually for egg laying, starting from the age of the beginning of the reproductive career (adult pullet). If it is a laying hen, it begins to lay eggs around the 5th/6th month of age. Depending on the breed it can be more or less inclined to become a hen.

And with the hen, we arrive at the adult stage of the animal. Here are hens of various breeds that happily scratch around outdoors.

Cockerel

Male, from the age of the beginning of the reproductive career up to about 6 months.

Free-Range Rooster

A method of sustainable poultry farming that allows the flock to roam free outdoors, for at least part of the day, instead of living in confinement housing and fed on corn, bran and oats.

Capon

Male chickens that have been castrated to improve the quality of its meat.

Cock

Male, starting from about 10 months (at this age, the reproductive career is at its peak of sexual maturity).

Curiosity

To understand if a chick will be a hen or a rooster, we can use some indicators:

1. Basic colors: it is a method that works quite well in the event that the bred poultry breed has clear distinctions between male and female, such as the different number of basic colors, the presence of spots on the crest or wattles only on one or the other sex (or spots on the plumage of the head) and the different streak of the plumage that already at the age of chickens and pullets could appear different;

2. Plumage growth speed: it is a technique that well works between same "brood" animals, in which it is possible to notice, starting from the first week, that the feathers of the females grow faster than the roosters' feathers;

3. Color of the crest: in chickens and pullets of many breeds the crest will begin to grow after about a month from birth (already as chicks) and, while in males it will begin to take on a reddish tint, in females it will still be yellow;

4. Dimensions: always with the same breed, starting from a few weeks of life, the cockerels differs from the female by its size and its longer legs;

5. Head shape: males heads have clearly visible angles (more angular and large) unlike females which have smaller and rounder heads;

6. Different temperament (an empirical method): enter the hen house and pretend to sneeze; while the males will stand still, the females will probably run away in every direction!

Nine Good Reasons

So let's start our list of "nine good reasons" to start a small breeding of some hens at home, with what is the fundamental reason and which, in the vast majority of cases, is the spring that triggers the purchase of the chicken coop and chickens, our chance to use fresh eggs practically every day of the year! A really good reason if we care about a healthy diet that respects animal health.

FRESH EGGS

Thanks to the small domestic chicken coop that you have built in your garden a few meters away from your home, with 4/5 good hatching hens, you will have availability of fresh and genuine eggs throughout the year, with which to create many and delicious recipes.

Eggs are a real super food, very rich in beneficial properties for our body, and having them just laid by happy hens and with a healthy diet is a really good way to follow a healthy daily diet.

CRUELTY FREE CHICKENS

The hens raised in your own garden, trying to best satisfy all their ethological needs, will certainly be "happy hens" that will live free in a good environment for them. By equipping a small family chicken coop, you will therefore make your contribution to the fight against large intensive farms, in favor of a supply of eggs that is more respectful of nature and the life of hens. Furthermore, by no longer buying eggs at the supermarket, you will save the environment from a lot of cardboard and plastic packaging.

LESS FOOD WASTE

In addition to giving us their precious eggs, chickens also help us to dispose of some of the wet food waste we produce; obviously the supply of "leftover food" must take place with the awareness of a correct diet for laying hens and of those that are poisonous foods for hens.

In addition, the daily diet of hens includes insects, spiders, larvae, ants, ticks (even small mice sometimes), and therefore, they help to keep under control the proliferation of these, often unwanted, little animals around the house.

NATURAL FERTILIZER

From the droppings hens, which are usually collected in a special compartment inside the chicken coop, it is possible, with an appropriate procedure, to create one of the best natural organic fertilizers, which can be used (with caution) to provide nutrients and energy to your plants and to your vegetables.

A GREAT WARNING SIGNAL

You will easy understand when a danger or a threat to your hens is appearing in your garden because of the various noises from the hen house; when they feel in danger or there is something upsetting them, they emit a very strong particular "cry", a sort of "natural alarm", which will alert you immediately, giving you the possibility to do something promptly and resolve the occurred situation (especially in case of enemies, also dogs).

PET THERAPY

They love to play and their antics can literally keep you entertained for hours. Despite of their bad bad reputation they are quite smart, they can even play instruments such as the xylophone.

They are also being widely used as therapy animals in different nations.

For these reasons, chickens offer significant therapeutic benefits for people of all ages and are proving a powerful therapeutic tool for those suffering from a lot of mental illnesses.

PEST CONTROL

Chickens love to eat icky and annoying bugs in the yard. They'll happily devour spiders, mosquitoes, ticks, beetles, crickets and also caterpillars. You will have zero mosquito bites and this is a very good news, for many people.

HEALTHY ANTI-STRESS HOBBY IN THE OPEN AIR

In a daily life increasingly linked to indoor spaces and hours at the computer, the fact of owning a domestic chicken coop in the garden, and therefore to keep it clean and tidy, will "force" us to spend some time outside in the garden at the open air, relaxing and releasing the stress of the day. The farming of laying hens in the garden is becoming increasingly popular among the executives of hi-tech companies in Silicon Valley, considered an ideal hobby to spend some time in nature and to "detoxify" from excess of hours spent in front of the monitors.

PETS

Chickens make great pets. They are very kind and gentle. When you raise and handle chickens from small chicks they will eat from your hand, sit in your lap, and follow you around the yard. They even come to you when you call and are early risers who like to go to bed just before dusk. They will come running when they see you coming.

They are lovely and you will adore take care of them, and so they will.

The Brooding Hen

If you are new to small chicken farm and have never faced the egg hatching period, you may encounter difficulties since you do not have the know-how of this business.

By following my advice you will have total control and will be able to better manage all the problems that may occur.

The definition of hen is very simple: hen that hatches eggs and raises the chicks. But the reality of things is much more complex and being a laying hen can be a very tiring job for a hen, long (in total even 3/4 months) and which takes away a lot of effort (in fact she stops laying eggs).

In hens, the instinct to hatch can depend on various factors such as genetic predisposition, health conditions and the environment in which they live.

Not all have this propensity, so if a female does not spontaneously become a hen it is absolutely not recommended to force her. Hatching is a very stressful period: facing it without being ready could lead the hen to weaken too much.

18

Some breeds are particularly inclined to perform the role of broods. Isa Brown, Plymouth Rock, Barnevelder, Australorp, Nacked Neck, Orpington and Silkie have exceptional hatching instincts.

However, remember that the common hens that populate our countryside are almost always good hens and will ensure you excellent broods! You can recognize a brooding hen, just observing her behavior. The hen will be ready to hatch only after laying a certain number of eggs, which varies from a minimum of 7 to a maximum of about 20.

At this point your hen will begin to stay in the nest for a long time, leaving it only a few minutes a day to eat and drink. In order to be sure and recognize without mistakes a brooding hen, you should get close and stroke it: most likely it will inflate the feathers of the back and emit a downward and prolonged sound, called clucking. Your hen may decide to hatch in the place where it usually lays eggs, however, its "roommates" may try to lay in her own nest. They could even annoy it to such an extent that it would abandon the hatching. We therefore recommend that you reserve a corner for the hen inside the chicken coop, where it can hatch in total tranquility.

Any container is suitable for the new nest, as long as it does not have too high sides and is filled abundantly with straw or dusted shavings. In this way, the temperature will remain constant and the hen will have less difficulty in heating the newborn chicks.

When the nest is ready you will have to move the hen. We advise you to do this at night, so as not to scare the expectant mother. By shedding light with a small flashlight, you will have to transfer the eggs to the new nest and then very carefully transport the hen too. Feeling the warmth of the eggs beneath her, the hen will continue to hatch them. The next morning, waking up in the new accommodation, he will behave as usual. In this very busy period, your hen needs a lot of energy and therefore a diet rich in proteins. His daily diet must include grains, fruits and vegetables. You should never run out of fresh, clean water, to which you could add a multivitamin. Some hens put so much effort into hatching that they stop feeding. If you notice that your hen is not eating, try to get her out of the nest: the lack of food seriously endangers her health!

BAD HABITS

Sometimes, our chickens get some bad propensities. Some mostly cause a disturbance, similar to egg-eating, while others can result serious harm to your flocks. In case that your chickens have bad habits and these are affecting your henhouse's quality life, it is imperative to make some changes.

Laying eggs on the floor

Laying eggs on the ground instead of the proper place is not such a big problem. Young hens, infact could run into this error due to inexperience and lack of guidance. Eggs on the floor not attended could be easily crush or or worse, it can lead other hens to peck at them. Furthermore, this behavior can be imitated by other hens creating further problems inside the hen house.

For this reason it is important that there are enough nesting boxes, one box for every 3/4 hens. Also, remember to collect the eggs left unattended and try to insert fake eggs in the nest so as to encourage the novices.

Egg-eating

This can become a nuisance as you no longer have your precious eggs available. This bad habit can start to involve the whole group looking for any available egg to peck it.

Unfortunately it is difficult to remedy this problem but it is possible to prevent it in some way for example by providing the hens with enough and comfortable nests for hatching, becoming quick to collect the laid eggs, providing the hens with the right diet with balanced calcium and protein intake. Furthermore, individuals who exhibit that bad behavior should be isolated.

If you continue to find broken eggs in the chicken coop, despite these precautions, try replacing the real eggs with fake eggs or painted stones; once you have taken the laid egg, replace it with a fake one so that the hen, biting it, will be convinced that it is not edible!

Plus, you can also play a small and harmless joke, that is, fill a real egg with mustard! Hens hate mustard and in a short time they will stop looking for it and pecking it.

In the Garden or Outdoors?

Having a small green space in the garden is great for starting laying hens. You can also raise them outdoors but remember that the hens must have a chicken coop (covered shelter) and a grazing area (your garden). In the chicken coop you will need to make sure to create nesting nests where the hens can feel safe and warm, away from the cold.

This is a list of the things you will need to effectively prepare a chicken coop in your garden and to be able to grow your chickens without problems (or almost):

- 4 months old hens already vaccinated;

- Drinking troughs equipped with a drip tray;

- Plastic boxes;

- Straw;

Chicken coop, shelter or cage. The size depends on the number of hens, we just tell you that the chicken coops equipped for 2/3 hens should measure at least 59 inches and be equipped with perches, nest for collecting eggs, drinking trough and a manger.

Before you can decide how many hens to acquire, you need to evaluate the space available and be able to give the hens the opportunity to roam freely in the area, in fact each of them will need at least 21 square feet of land.

CHAPTER TWO

Raising Chickens

Raising Terrace Poultry

Numerous chicken breeds are superbly appropriate for run lawn. Selecting the correct breed for your patio rush exclusively depends on the poultry manager's needs. Chicken breeds can be separated into two essential classes: winged animals for meat and feathered creatures for eggs.

For picking a chicken breed for your terrace run, the poultry specialists at Smallholder Magazine stated the following:

"All breeds and types of hen produce similar healthy eggs, either smaller on account of bantams or bigger for specific breeds. Regardless of whether they are white, dark-colored, khaki, or blue, nutritional contents are the same. Some pure breeds lay superior eggs relative to others, and within the pure breed, there are certain laying strains' that produce a greater number of eggs than different birds of that breed.

For sheer dependability on laying eggs, pick half breeds. There are some beautiful backyard halves now, for example: the appealing 'Bluebell' and the 'Dotted' that lays light dark colored eggs. Yet, I've kept the two crossovers and thoroughbreds for quite a long time, and these two types of birds have impressive characteristics."

To get more information on breeds and to get information on reproducers and incubation facilities, you may need to visit any Poultry Association in your vicinity. On the other hand, fantastic assets are abundant on the web.

As an alternative to purchasing eggs and grown-up birds from an incubator, eggs or winged animals can also be bought legitimately from poultry managers. Oftentimes, smallholders exchange or sell chickens in the wake of laying season. To find out fowls available for exchange or deal, check poultry classifieds sites.

TOP CHICKEN BREEDS

These are some of the most famous breeds:

Isa Brown

ISA Brown is the most common and best known laying hen (hybrid). The breed was developed and patented by a French company in 1978 for optimum egg production and since then their popularity has grown to great heights. Among all the species it is certainly the most widespread in chicken coops, also for its extraordinary ability as an egg producer. The average is about 300 eggs per year, of medium size and light brownish shell color. It is a very quiet, sweet and loving hen and has a good resilience, since the hatching activity requires a lot of energy. It has an important sexual dimorphism: the white chicks are male while the females are light brown. It is a hen that resists quite well even in harsh winters.

Plymouth Rock

The Plymouth Rock is a heavy breed, originally from the American city of Plymouth, to which it owes its name; at the beginning of 1874 it was called Plymouth Rock Barrato, to indicate the signs present on the plumage. They are large and long-lived animals. Sociable animals, easily tamed, robust and resistant; they do not need large spaces, even though they love to scratch freely.

You don't need tall fences for them, because they don't fly well. They lay an average of 200 cream-colored eggs each year. Plymouth Rock hens have a hatching instinct, which can be limited with regular egg collection. Chicks develop feathers early and are very suitable for children, thanks to their docile disposition.

New Hampshire

This dual-purpose chicken breed was born from the direct selection of another historic american breed, the Rhode Island. It is an excellent laying hen, rustic and good scratcher, which lays 180 - 220 pink shell eggs a year. It is tawny, with black tail and flight feathers and some traces of black also on the fur.

As a medium sized bird, they can be quite food aggressive and are willing to push and shove flock mates out of the way; certainly not a good thing if you have shy, docile breeds already. However you can try to reduce this bullying behavior by having several feeding stations that are spread apart from each other.

Obviously their personalities will vary greatly so be aware they can be anywhere from docile and lovable all the way to unfriendly and aggressive.

Australorp

Australorp hens share with the Orpington breed the rather robust, rounded and heavy tonnage, which over time has also made them famous as a meat breed. The recognized colors are 3: black, edged blue and white. The black Australorp is by far the most widespread. One of the most important qualities of Australorp is that it produces a high quantity of eggs. The Australorp laying hen begins to lay at 5 months of age and is one of the most productive breeds of all but unfortunately has a low propensity for hatching.

Orpington

It is an English breed originally from Kent, including several varieties with different origins.

Selected by the English William Cook in 1886. The name derives from the village where Cook lived. It has a considerable weight and is used for the production of white skinned meat. It lays eggs with a reddish shell.

We are used to seeing mainly white-shelled eggs on supermarket counters, or exceptionally brown-colored eggs. But wouldn't you like to add some very special eggs to the table, of the deepest chocolate brown or a pale sky blue? So know that there are two magnificent breeds of laying hens that can help you: the French Marans and the South American Araucana.

Marans

It lays eggs with a very dark shell, the darker the shell the greater the value of the egg; in France, competitions are organized to evaluate this characteristic. Did you know they were also the James Bond character's favorite breakfast eggs?

Araucana

The Araucana is unmistakable: it has a small pea-like crest, sports showy tufts of mustache-like feathers near the ears and does not have a tail! But in addition to these unique physical characteristics, what makes her special is the color of her eggs, a magnificent light blue.

There are so many breeds to make your chicken coop unique, but these are certainly among the most productive and interesting.

Laying and Incubating Eggs

Once the eggs have been laid, you may choose to hatch them using mechanical incubators or use the old brooding chicken method. To incubate the eggs naturally it is necessary to have a hen capable of hatching for the time necessary for the brooding, that is three weeks. The eggs should be placed in a nest filled with soft, dust-free bedding. If you have more than a dozen eggs, you may want to keep some of them aside or incubate them artificially.

Some breeds are naturally prone to hatching, while others are not at all. The best hens are those of Asil, Barnevelder, Brahma, Cochin, Delaware, Dominque, Dorking, Faverolle, Holland, Japanese, Jersey Giant, Maran, New Hampshire Red, Old English Game, Orpington, Polish, Plymouth Rock, Rhode Island Red , Silkie, Sussex, Welsummer and Wyandotte. If you have hens of a modern breed not bred to hatch eggs, we advise you not to force it. Even if hatching begins, she may leave the eggs before 21 days, so before hatching.

HOW TO MAKE THE HEN BECOME A BROODING HEN

If you like the idea of letting nature take its course, and you have the right breed of hens, then you will need a hen that sits on the eggs for the time they need to hatch. You can encourage her by leaving artificial eggs in the nest but you should not force the chicken to become a hen. Fake eggs look the same as real ones and can be used to induce the hen to hatch.

Hatching is a difficult and extremely demanding time for any hen: only an animal in perfect physical condition will try to hatch.

The hen may visit the nest from time to time, until she decides to stay there for 24 hours. At that point the hatching instinct takes control and you can substitute real eggs for fake ones, letting the hen do its job. It would be better (especially in the case of very exuberant roosters) that our hen could be in a suitable environment, to successfully complete her brood and not be excessively disturbed. The chosen place should be in dim light, in order to give tranquility to the future mother; moreover it is necessary to immediately think of some type of fence to isolate it from other animals.

The new nest must be well repaired and will consist of a small box or basket with sides about 10-15 cm high (excellent many baskets for fruit), and lined inside with a good, soft and welcoming substrate. In my opinion, the best substrate is made up of shavings used as animal bedding: in addition to being very hygienic and retaining moisture, it is also quite economical and can be used later as a litter for chicks. Chips are a great choice as long as they aren't too small or dusty. It won't hurt the chicks if they decide to start eating the shavings, and in most cases, they'll determine it doesn't taste as great, but to be safe, a large shave would probably be the best option. Also, you can try mixing powdered tobacco with shavings, as the nicotine contained in it can act as a natural insecticide against the many external parasites of the hen itself.

The hen should be moved at night, because otherwise, it could become extremely stressed and decide to abandon the brood. Just take some of its eggs and place them in the new nest while still warm, then move the hen inside the new nest. The fact that it is dark and the heat beneath her will soothe her and she will feel like she has never moved.

Make sure the hen eats and drinks enough while brooding by placing bowls for water and feed approximately 12 inches away. In this way the hen will not have to go too far from the nest and will be able to defecate outside of it.

Eggs ought to be turned about 3-5 times each day. Insufficient turning can lead to distorted chicks as the incipient organism could stick to the side of an egg.

The hen can stay in the cage with the chicks for thirty days, then will be removed and will return with the other chickens; the chicks will remain in the cage instead until 2 /3 months, until they can be able to defend themselves well enough or escape effectively.

If you prefer an artificial incubator you may need a nurse to take care of the newborn chicks. Always at night you take some chickens and put them under the hen, removing the eggs at the same time: often a hen will accept to become a mother even just a few days from the beginning of the hatching. However, it is not guaranteed that the hen decides to keep the new "adopted children", in fact it could also decide to kill them.

CHECK THE EGGS

When the chicken becomes a brooding hen, it shows excessive attachment to the eggs. Try to keep the other hens away from the nest and not to disturb it as mentioned before. Otherwise, you will hear it making strange sounds and trying to peck you.

The ideal temperature for chicken eggs is 102°F (38°C). Moistness is additionally essential for an egg to incubate. Chicken eggs are normally kept at 58-60% humidity for the initial 18 days. During the most recent long periods of hatching, chicken eggs generally sit in 65% humidity. That steady temperature can be given by natural hatching using an agonizing hen or fake brooding by means of an incubator.

The process that leads to the birth of a chick will only trigger when the hen has sat on top of the eggs. This means that they will all hatch together. The hen turns the eggs regularly during incubation, in order to ensure that the embryos do not stick to the shell membrane, and that the temperature is evenly distributed. The mother hen hatches for 21 days, leaving the nest only for short periods (about 20 minutes), when she needs to eat, drink or take a walk to stretch her legs.

After 18 days, the chicks will begin to force the shell from the inside to break it. You can hear your hen clucking to encourage the birth of the young. It will take 3 days for all the babies to fully emerge from the eggs. Eggs, despite being laid at different times, bring forth around the same time.

IMPROVING LAYING

The bird's age, breed, and shedding period are responsible for its capacity to lay eggs. Certain chicken breeds were reproduced to lessen the activity of brooding conduct and increase laying capacity. If a poultry manager needs to keep chicken for eggs, it is imperative to select a chicken breed that exhibits significant levels of egg generation.

Isa Brown chickens are well known with patio proprietors because of their high number of egg production.

To expand egg production, brooding conduct must be diminished. At the point when an egg-laying hen shows brooding conduct, the hen can be isolated from the remainder of the herd and put in the henhouse. Removing the hens from visual and physical incitement as found in their original home and settling them will help reduce this conduct. Also, it will help counteract laying hens from watching and embracing the broody conduct of their group mates. The hens ought to be held in this confinement pen for seven to 10 days before moving them back to the laying pen.

Longer days, or extended times of light, empower egg-laying. Hens usually lay more eggs during seasons with longer days. As the length days reduce, hens start to show broodier conduct. During these shorter days, after the normal rearing season, hens start to shed their feathers. Since shedding requires a lot of vitality, hens reduce their egg generation. To keep up typical egg creation, hens require around 12-14 hours of light, which can be given artificially when days become shorter.

A pullet (a female chicken less than one-year-old), which is chosen to turn into an egg-laying hen ought to have an eating regimen that comprises of 12-16% protein. Matured egg-laying hens ought to have an eating routine high in calcium and minerals. Nutritional maladies can happen in egg-laying hens if they aren't furnished with a satisfactory eating routine. The ideal is to place the manger and drinker about half a meter away from the nest, in order to encourage the hen to get up for a few minutes to be able to feed and drink (and perhaps defecate outside the nest).

THE CANDLING

The candling of the eggs is the operation that allows us, illuminating with a light source the inside of the incubated egg, to understand whether embryonic development is going well or not. It does not damage the embryo and does not compromise the outcome of incubation. Indeed, it is very important because it allows us to eliminate cracked eggs or dead embryos that would risk breaking or rotting, compromising all other healthy eggs.

To recognize whether an egg has been fertilized or not, it is necessary to note the center of the embryo and its blood vessels, which will appear to your eyes as a dark point from which small veins depart.

A fertilized egg is heavier than an unfertilized one, so you just need to weigh it before and after to see a possible change in weight. However, it must be borne in mind that if the egg is in an incubator, the heat will tend to evaporate the water inside and make it lighter.

Lodging Backyard Chickens

You have just had the impulse to build your own chicken coop; everything is clear in your head, and there is a strong desire to have excellent laying hens by your side that can lay fresh quality eggs every day for delicious recipes, also contributing to the disposal of food waste from your table.

Therefore, having taken this decision, there are two essential checks to do:

- the availability of suitable space for the construction of your chicken coop, respecting the ethological needs and the well-being of the hens housed;

- compliance with current legislation regarding domestic chicken coops.

Once these two checks have been made, it will then be possible to indulge in the design of the chicken coop, which can be built either by assembling the prefabricated kits on the market or by self-building original structures with recycled materials.

THE CLOSED AND OPEN SPACES OF THE CHICKEN COOP

The most important thing before proceeding is to evaluate the location of the chicken coop. This is a very reasoned choice to avoid bad disappointments. The chicken coop should be built in an area very well exposed to the sun: the heat favors egg laying and the sun prevents diseases.

Ideally, each chicken or hen would need one square meter in the covered shelter and 21 sq ft of grazing area. In this area we will have to take into account that the hens will have to be able to scratch, peck, scrape the ground and graze in search of food, gravel, insects, worms and fresh grass (to guarantee their well-being and therefore the nutritional quality of the eggs).

The correct management of the hygiene of the hen house will be essential, which basically translates into the correct sizing and proper management of the spaces inside the house and in particular of the roost (under which the nocturnal manure will be collected).

The movement of animals stimulates their metabolism and immune defenses; optimal density values have been identified to be followed according to the location of the spaces and the age of the animals.

Internal space:

10 chicks/chickens (first 2 months of life) X 10 sq ft

4 hens/chickens (after 2 months of age) X 10 sq ft

Providing the hens with an outdoor space is very important, as it makes the animals free to move and feel psychologically more free, with a positive impact on production. The outdoor spaces are healthy and beneficial if we take into account the load of animals per unit of surface. Furthermore, outdoor spaces are better when they are equipped with trees or hedges to allow shelter in difficult weather conditions, such as in summer to favor the presence of shade or during the rains to shelter. Another good thing about open spaces can be the growth of herbaceous cover that is spontaneous or grown with clover-like crops, which the hens are very fond of.

CHICKEN COOP

Dig the foundation at least 11 inches tall and then start building the walls at least 3 feet high, leaving room for a door. Use a roofing plate to make the roof so that they are protected from the elements. The fence is used to prevent foxes and other predators from doing damage. Bury a net at least 15 inches, so they can't dig holes, and raise it about 6.5 feet (more on this later).

The main purpose of the closed housing of a hen house is to protect cocks and hens not only from possible attacks of external predators, but also in general from atmospheric agents. Specifically, the walls will have to insulate from possible frosts or air currents in winter and from too high temperatures in summer. Whether it is made of wood or metal, the shelter structure must be draught-proof, but above all it must guarantee a good thermal insulation both in the heat and in the cold. To thermally insulate the floor of the shelter it may be useful to keep it raised from the ground. There must also be good natural lighting useful for the general well-being of the hens, as well as small windows that will allow the entry of clean and fresh air.

THE OPEN SPACE FOR GRAZING HENS

The open space around the small house must be designed according to the specific conditions of the garden or area and land available, as well as the type of breed reared. Obviously, there must be enough space to graze.

In this sense it is important to specify that the types of chicken coops on the market with a small fenced area (called "run") are equipped with this space in which to keep our hens only for short periods, for example in the morning (before you go to open them for grazing) or in particular conditions (to keep them safe).

These small fences absolutely cannot be replaced with the possibility of grazing freely in a larger space (precisely at least 10 sq meter per hen); even more so, in the case of a mobile chicken coop on wheels, we must not fall into the error of thinking that our 2, 3, or 4 hens can remain closed in the space of 10,7 sq ft or a little more.

The greater the grazing area available to your hens, the lower their impact on the habitat will be (you could also think about creating temporary fences or moving your chicken coop in such a way as to alternate grazing in different areas for a few months).

In the event that the chicken coop is built in a context without hen predators (for example an urban context) and you decide to raise a breed of hens with a calm temperament and not very inclined to fly (such as the Moroseta, the Cochinchina, the Brahma or the Orpington), a garden fence may be sufficient, or fences of the same height as garden fences (about 40-60 inches).

Where there is a problem of predators, it will be necessary to provide special fences (because predators could easily and sadly kill all your animals) and make sure that during the night the roost is totally safe and impenetrable from the outside.

In the event that in the area there is the presence of predators such as foxes or weasels (and never underestimate the danger of mice and rats, especially for chicks and young specimens), it is strongly recommended to provide a strip of anti-excavation net of about 20 inches wide outside the base of the fence, even simply at ground level or buried up to 12 inches deep (the important thing is that there is a 90 ° bend because at that point the predators will start to dig and will not find way to overcome the corner; without this point of curvature, by digging, predators may be able to pass it from below).

Another system to adopt, in the case of predators who might try to climb the fence net and enter from above, is the anti-predator protrusion; or a protrusion towards the outside of the fence (also inclined) with an overhang of about 10-30 cm.

A special fence may also be necessary, however, to avoid the "fleeing hens" phenomenon; some breeds (such as the free range Leghorn hen) are able to make very high jumps and in some cases some real small flights (unless you proceed with the extreme remedies of cutting the flight feathers); the fence must therefore be high enough or, even better, also closed on the high top side. The "top" closure is necessary if you live in areas where birds of prey float.

METHODS TO PREVENT HENS FROM FLYING

As we have therefore seen so far in this article, in certain contexts the ability of hens to take flight represents a condition of total freedom of movement which is certainly synonymous with well-being, but in many other cases (domestic or urban chicken coops) this ability is turns into a real problem, which needs to find a solution.

The use of tethers that immobilize the wings creating not only annoyance and stress for the hen, but also causing dangerous gangrene risks (because they can tighten too much) is definitely a practice to be avoided at all.

Instead, among the possible solutions, the most demanding from a time-cost point of view is certainly the 360 ° closure of the hen house with anti-escape nets; unfortunately the result is the construction of an effective large cage (including also the space for grazing) which, however large, still remains a cage. Depending on the size to be fenced, it may not be necessary to close the 'roof' as well (the height of the perimeter network tends to vary from one and a half to two and a half meters).

In this case, it is also good to pay attention to the presence of any "springboards" within the fenced area, which could make even the highest fence in vain, such as boulders, joists, branches, walls, etc. If it is not possible to eliminate such "trampolines", then the closure of the 'roof' should be considered, which can also have the function of both protecting food from the incursions of other birds (especially pigeons and doves if you are in an urban context), and to avoid attacks from predators of the sky (such as hawks, owls and buzzards, which are a danger not only for chicks but also for adult specimens; magpies, crows and crows are instead greedy for eggs, and usually do not attack the adults).

Curiosity

Do chickens fly or don't fly? In general, we can say that the hens are not able to fly as they are unable to cover in flight more than 300 inches, even if the lighter and more rustic breeds (such as the Leghorn hens) can reach more long distances.

We could also say that hens do not fly because they do not actually need them, but they can take short flights when needed, for example to jump over a fence or onto a tree branch in search of food or to sleep, either out of necessity. escape from some predator.

They usually fly short, with very fast wing flapping (noisy and without gliding), in a straight line and at a short height from the ground.

CLIP THE HEN'S WINGS

Another possible solution is the topping of the wings, or the "trimming" of the flight feathers, a method from which the expression "clipping the wings" comes from, or making it physically (or metaphorically) impossible to take flight.

Beyond the initial impression, the clipping of the wings is not an operation that causes pain to our hens, in fact it can be equivalent to giving our hair a trim. The remiges wings, as well as our hair, grow back when the feathers are moulted and this could possibly allow us to carry out a test.

The topping of the wings is however a controversial practice, whose pros and cons should be evaluated case by case. For some this practice represents a sort of animal abuse, but where it is aimed at protecting hens from far worse risks, it can be considered legitimate.

On the other hand, plucking the flight feathers should be avoided, because the plucking - unlike the well-done topping - causes pain and stress to the animal.

The topping of the wings is therefore an effective and non-stressful method to avoid letting the hens fly but it certainly has an important contraindication, namely the inability for the animal to jump/fly even where it was necessary, for example to escape from a predator, and it is therefore important to make the appropriate assessments before proceeding.

Predators

How do we defend our hens from predator attacks? And what are the most dangerous predators to watch out for? For those who own a small domestic chicken coop in an urban area, within their garden, it is likely that there is no need to defend the hens from real predators.

MICE AND RATS

Rats are a danger to both chicks and adults and they are, unfortunately, a common problem. These rodents easily find food inside the chicken coop and getting rid of it is not at all easy as they are often very wary of poisoned baits and, in any case, they learn very quickly to recognize and avoid them.

Mice are dangerous in many ways: they are carriers of diseases that are dangerous to humans and chickens, they gnaw wood in chicken coops or chicken houses, break eggs to eat them, and sometimes even kill chicks.

For these reasons it is absolutely necessary to eradicate them from our chicken coop as soon as possible, especially because they are really quick to form a colony and reproduce, thus becoming a real scourge out of control.

Like all animals, mice also follow their instinct, which is to gnaw, eat the food of other animals and soil the chicken coop. Mice are not at fault and therefore do not deserve to be killed with bait or traps (unless it becomes a public health concern).

A first important precaution is to pay close attention to the remains of food left around by the hens at the end of the day and therefore try to keep our domestic chicken coop as clean as possible, giving the right food doses so that the leftovers are few, and use non-accessible feeders (e.g. foot feeders).

In this regard, I suggest an effective solution to make food unreachable for mice, creating a raised floor of about 40 inches from the ground through a single central stake stuck in the ground, which will also be sprinkled with fat.

In this way, the hens will still be able to reach the upper floor to eat with a small flourish, while the mice will be unable to do so, and they will have to be content with only a few crumbs or grains of grain fallen to the ground!

There are also ultrasonic deterrents for mice and rats which emit ultrasounds at wavelengths that are unbearable for the hearing of rodents, but in no way harmful. Humans and chickens do not hear these sounds, so they are not disturbed by them, while mice will immediately leave the area. You can place the machines in certain areas of the house to cover as much area as possible.

I propose two other solutions for rodent control:

-Take chestnut flour (of which mice are very greedy) and mix it with masonry plaster powder (approximate quantity: 2/3 flour and 1/3 plaster); this mix is placed in small bowls in places that cannot be reached by other animals (ideal are those that host poisoned baits and which are therefore also easily found on the market); wait a few days and the mice will have all (or almost all) been eliminated. The dead mouse in this way is not dangerous for other animals as the chalk has already acted in the rat's stomach and no longer reacts. A 100% ecological and very effective solution.

- It will seem trivial or maybe it can make you smile but having cats can really prove to be an excellent solution. Not of domestic cats of course, but country cats, which constantly live out in the open space, and you will feed them only once a day (during the period of the presence of the mice), so that they are also pushed to look for it elsewhere.

This would seem to be one of the most effective solutions and obviously also in this case 100% ecological. There is even a proverb, which says: "Better cats than rats!".

PS: in our personal experience the cat has proved to be the most effective of the solutions against a small invasion by mice; in about a couple of weeks it took over 10 and eliminated the colony. Small problem: in several cases, instead of killing them on the spot, he took them home still alive, to show us proudly his trophy.

THE DOG

Beware of dogs. Even those of the house, in fact, could attack and kill the hens. It will therefore be good to get your dogs used to the presence of chickens from an early age, so that they become their guardians and not their predators. It would be better to feed the dog without the presence of the chickens because they throw themselves headlong and the dog, if not used, could get nervous and react. Also try to prevent the hen from bothering the dog. In fact, it could happen that this one wants to try to claim its territory, and tries to attack the dog. In that case, it is the hen that must be turned away.

THE "NEIGHBORS"

The last "predator" that in the urban area could prove to be the most fearful of all, is the one represented by some neighbor! Even if it's legal in your urban or suburban area to keep chickens, the law may require your neighbors 'approval and continued tolerance.

Try to always keep the chicken coop clean and tidy, both internally and externally, and that it is aesthetically decent. Make sure that the hens have as little cackle as possible and above all give eggs to the neighbors. All great attention to transform the potential "human predator" into an enthusiastic supporter of your poultry passion.

Even if roosters are legal, consider doing without them. its noise can be annoying for some people who might complain.

Chicken Predators in Rural and Wooded Areas

A completely different thing, however, for those who live in the countryside, in wooded areas or in any case outside and far from inhabited centers. Building and maintaining a chicken coop in this situation is much more complex and protecting hens from predator attacks means a lot more work. We no longer have to worry about the likely irritable neighbor but, especially at night, there will be various and different carnivorous animals that will try to attack our hens. Let's see who they are and how to protect themselves.

THE FOX

The fox is shrewd and intelligent, attracted to the smell of chickens, especially in spring, when it has to feed its cubs. He loves to hunt especially after sunset and before sunrise. The relationships of foxes with humans have a long history: if their predatory nature makes them the enemy of small farmers, others consider them very useful because of their activity against rodents and other animals that can damage crops.

Many think they can protect their hens with a simple net, but then they are mocked; when a fox finds an obstacle, in fact, it does not have many scruples and often manages to get around it: most of the times they climb (these animals manage to overcome nets up to 2 meters high without major problems), still others dig the land under the barrier in question to create an underground passage.

To be smarter than them you will have to be the first to dig: when you install your net, in fact, it will be necessary to create a small ditch at least 20 inches deep along the entire perimeter of the fence. Once the work is completed, the net will be placed and planted in the ground giving it an "L" shape, towards the outside of the chicken coop. By doing so, not even the most indomitable of foxes will be able to sneak in.

However, there are other ways to protect your chicken coop from foxes and keep these predators away without harming them. By exploiting their fears, for example with water which is a good deterrent for many animals, which tend to flee like hell if they are reached by a jet. Precisely for this reason it is possible to find on the market water animal chasers equipped with a motion sensor: these devices are planted in the ground and as soon as they detect the passage of a possible predator, it repels it with a short spray.

In addition to this solutions, having one or more dogs loose on the property during the night is also an excellent way to counteract the fox's approaching the chicken coop and its undisturbed operation. In fact, if dogs, as we have seen above, can sometimes turn into predators, in the vast majority of cases it is they who guard the hens and the chicken coop, and save them from the attack of wild carnivores.

Curiosity

In England there is an ancient tradition for which Welsh Corgy Pembroke dogs are used against predators. Even today, in many English farms, these specimens are used, which are deadly against foxes and stone martens. Here is a video that features this cute and efficient little dog.

THE MARTEN

The Beech Marten, the Weasel and the Marten, although all mustelids, differ in some aesthetic aspects that distinguish them, but their way of acting is very similar. They usually attack chickens when they have no other animals to hunt.

One of the first measures to be adopted in case of presence of Mustelids near a hen house, is to keep clean the environment where the hens live, ensuring not to leave rotten food or residues from the bad smell around the fence that delimits the hen house.

To defend the chicken coop against mustelids it is necessary to create a fence with very narrow 0.4 inch (max 1) meshes (with the characteristics that we have already mentioned in the paragraph dedicated to the fox), and always check that there are no gaps or accesses of any kind; even better if we can close all the hens in a completely sealed night shelter (concrete base, roof and ventilation slots protected by a sturdy net). The weasels, for example, have an extraordinary ability to cross even the smallest openings; this is one of the characteristics that make this animal extremely dangerous for the safety of the hens present in a hen house. One of the strategies most used by farmers who have problems with martens is to "raise" the chicken coop off the ground by building the floor of the structure so that it is above the ground.

If these animals, despite all the precautions taken, have not yet given up attacking the chicken coop and the poor hens, then it may be necessary to take real traps.

The predatory instinct of stone martens is activated by movement; for this reason, often and willingly, only one of them can kill even more prey at a time, excited by the agitation of the hens who, frightened, begin to run inside the chicken coop, thus feeding the hunger of the marten.

Another additional deterrent may be spraying the environment with anti-mustelide sprays found on the market.

THE RAPTORS

Many areas, especially hills and mountainous areas, can be hunting grounds for birds of prey, even very large and powerful ones (hawks and eagles). In this case it will obviously be necessary to keep our hens in the shelter of an aerial net or, during the day, use bells or mobile chicken coops, in order to place the poultry in always green pasture areas but still protected from attacks from above (at night, a more robust and safe hospitalization is always recommended). To give hens safety and shelter against attacks from the sky, it is also a good idea to insert small trees, bushes and low shrubs within the perimeter of the enclosure, under which the hens can hide or shelter in the event of an attack by a bird of prey.

SNAKES

Snakes can be extremely useful, as they are very effective in containing parasite populations. However, there are many species that quite happily eat eggs, hatching chicks, or even adult chickens if the snake is large enough.

In case of problems related to a habitual frequentation of snakes near the hen house and the pasture area, a fairly effective natural remedy could be to include a couple of turkeys in the poultry group.

Remember to keep the grass and vegetation outside well maintained. Most snakes don't like being too exposed outdoors and try to attack areas where they can be well hidden, such as tall grass, bushy shrubs, or even areas where lots of dead leaves on the ground can hide them.

Another all-natural remedy is to make a repellent with olive oil, cinnamon sticks and cloves. The smell of the spices must be very intense so we abound with cinnamon and cloves and let them macerate in a container in the dark for several days. Once ready, it will be spread along the boundaries of the fence and around the chicken coop, repeating the treatment several times after a few days.

Food

There is also a lot of other information to know to manage your chicken coop right from the start without making mistakes that could in some way, unintentionally, damage the wellness of your hens.

PROPER FEEDING OF LAYING HENS

Hens are notoriously omnivores and they will throw themselves on whatever food is offered to them, but we must be careful not to risk missing some fundamental components for proper nutrition.

As for us humans, each hen has a different nutritional requirement, which is determined by age, weight, sex, rearing method and time of year. Below are some general principles to be respected and adapted to each individual reality.

During the day, they constantly search for food (this activity, which we commonly call "scratching", is also a decisive anti-stress factor for them) and a large part of the daily food intake is the result of this meticulous sounding of the soil. It is important that the garden is covered with grass and wild plants but also small insects and earthworms, for a very important protein intake of excellent quality.

In order not to discourage them from scratching, the best times to provide them with food in the mangers (birdcages and racks) are mid-day and before dusk, in order to facilitate the afternoon nap of "after lunch" and sleep at night.

The chickens are attracted by more or less anything and each of them has its own specific preferences in certain foods.

The balanced diet of an adult hen requires a protein intake of 16% and it is therefore crucial to guarantee them this percentage; it is important to realize that providing only grains or just herbs and plants does not mean ensuring a correct and balanced diet.

WHAT HENS NEED TO EAT TO STAY HEALTHY

The hen's diet must be various and adapted to the biological phase or the time of year. It has to be based on their organism and physiology. They can eat grains, protein legumes, oil seeds, fresh grass and vegetables and elements rich in calcium.

Grains

About 35% of a balanced diet is made up of grains. It will necessary to provide them with a good intake of carbohydrates by ensuring the right doses of wheat, oats, barley, corn, sorghum, millet, rye, rice, spelled, quinoa, etc. In addition to the aforementioned whole grains, we could also prepare mash with the flours or small brans of all the grains listed.

Grain legumes

The contribution of proteins is decisive, made possible by the addition of a good amount of broken protein pea, field bean and broken whole soy. Various preparations with a high protein content are available on the market: among these the "feed for chicks" (with 23% protein content) and the "core" (based on soy). Other possible protein sources could be fly baits (70% protein) or mulberry leaves (20% protein). Wheat and bran contain only 8% protein.

Oil seeds

Other possible food to supplement the diet of our laying hens can be oil seeds (added in a percentage of 15% -25%), such as hemp, flax seeds and sunflower (chickens in particular enjoy black oil sunflower seeds and there are many pros associated with their consumption). Sunflower seeds are particularly high in levels of Vitamin "E", known to be vital for the poultry immune system and a protector against diseases like coccidiosis, e.coli and bronchitis; protein (this a great boost for chickens at times of stress such as moulting and cold weather); Oil as the high levels of linoleic acid increases weight and sets chickens up for the winter months and adds to the nutritional value (and weight) of eggs; antioxidants, another boost to the the immune system.

Fresh greens and grass

Vitamins are present in fresh grass and vegetables (avoid celery, parsley and cauliflower). It is important that the herbs and vegetables are fresh, not dry, not wilted (because they are indigestible), not moldy (because they are toxic) and not cooked. They love the leaves of black cabbage, savoy cabbage, rapeseed and other similar vegetables. The ideal would be to prepare a "manger" in which to place grass and vegetables so that they can be nibbled and not stepped on (for example, hung from a stake, a net or a branch, about 15 inches from the ground). In the summer, watermelon and melon seeds are highly appreciated.

Calcium rich elements

Another element to be taken into extreme consideration in the case of laying hens is the need for foods containing calcium, essential for the formation of hard and resistant eggshells.

Calcium is present both in pebbles, in sand, in snail shells or seashells, but it can also be made available with sunflower oil seeds and with a mix of dry bread, cheese and legumes (it is integrated in the feeding of hens usually with the grit). Calcium is obviously present, in high concentration, also in the shell of the eggs themselves, but giving it to the hens may not be entirely indicated as they could then pass, by association, to peck their own egg just laid. If we decide to give it anyway, it is good to grind it very finely and mix it with other foods.

Another food that can sometimes be crushed into the feed to provide calcium is cuttlefish bone.

Hens are very fond of leftovers from the canteen and from the kitchen: leftover pasta, risotto, meat, skins and vegetable scraps.

Warning: these delicacies must be considered a greedy addition and NOT the basis of their diet. Some foods would be low in nutrients or even toxic, with consequences for their health.

HELP THE DIGESTION OF THE HENS WITH "GRINDING ELEMENTS"

Another important aspect to take into consideration is digestive physiology. The hens have no teeth, and the ingested food is stored intact as well as swallowed in the goiter (a sort of dilation of the esophagus that we can see significantly enlarged at the end of a meal or at the end of the day). In the goiter, a first enzymatic digestion takes place with mixing and maceration. The food then passes into the glandular stomach (where gastric juices intervene) and then into the muscular stomach. In the muscular stomach it is crucial that there is the presence of "grinding elements" such as pebbles, sand, snail shells or shells; these elements are crucial in helping complete digestion and absorption of the vitamins found in fresh herbs and vegetables. it will therefore be necessary to ensure that there is availability, both in the pasture and in the feed (the latter must have the most heterogeneous shape and consistency possible; a mixture of chopped oyster shells called 'grit' is available on the market).

WHAT CHICKENS SHOULD NOT EAT

Knowing what the hen eats is very important both for their health and for ours, that we feed on their eggs. First of all, it is good to make it clear that hens, like all other animals, know very well how to distinguish by themselves, thanks to an instinct that has formed and evolved over millennia, what they can peck and what is better to avoid.

An experience common to all those who have hens free to scratch around in the uncultivated lawn is to notice how some spontaneous plants are literally stormed and totally stripped by the hens, while others are totally ignored, or just "tasted", only to be abandoned. The same thing certainly happens with mushrooms and other products of the earth; hens are capable of self-management in choosing what is good for them and what to avoid. Even with regard to more domestic hens, raised in family chicken coops, and therefore that may perhaps have lost some of that primordial instinct, we have never heard of cases in which one of them has felt ill (or died) for having spontaneously ingested some vegetable that is harmful or poisonous to her.

However, there are plants and flowers that are toxic to our hens and therefore, if you really want to be 100% sure that nothing can happen, here is the list of herbs that you should avoid having in the spaces used for hens: ranunculus, narcissus, delphinium , foxglove, horse chestnut, hyacinth, hydrangea, ivy, lupine, oleander, rhododendron, rhubarb, tulip, wisteria and yew.

FOUR TOXIC FOODS TO NEVER GIVE TO OUR CHICKENS

Raw dried beans

They are known to be poisonous to chickens. Any beans that have not been cooked properly are potentially lethal to our chickens. The problem is that beans contain a toxin called phytohemagglutinin which is very dangerous and even a small amount can put our poultry at serious risk. Therefore, it is absolutely forbidden to use dry and raw beans and to keep any bean plant away from chickens. To make them safe, it is necessary to soak them for several hours, throw away the soaking water, rinse them well and then boil them for at least 15 minutes. At this point, if desired, even the hens could eat them without running any danger, but our advice is to avoid them anyway.

Moldy fruit or vegetables

Although not all molds are toxic, especially for those that form on fruit and vegetables, it is not possible to distinguish between harmless and toxic ones, and therefore it is better to avoid the problem and not give the hens any spoiled or moldy food.

In particular, the mold that is also created on corn, nuts and apples is very likely to contain aflatoxin, one of the most toxic and carcinogenic substances in existence.

Therefore, in light of this, always check carefully that the corn and other grains that you give to your hens are stored in dry places, as humidity favors the development of mold.

Potatoes, aubergines and green tomatoes

It is best to avoid feeding potatoes, aubergines and green tomatoes (not ripe) to our hens as they contain solanine. Potato peels, in particular, contain a lot of it, so don't even throw them in organic compost if your hens have free access to it. Solanine is greatly reduced with cooking but our advice is to avoid feeding the hens even boiled potatoes. Once the tomatoes have ripened and become very red, they almost completely lose solanine and therefore in theory they could also be given to the hens (always in small doses). However, it should be borne in mind that the acidity of the tomato reduces the body's ability to absorb calcium (essential for hens), and therefore it is necessary to use great care even with ripe tomatoes.

Chocolate

In fact, chocolate is very bad for our hens because it contains theobromine, which is also harmful to cats and dogs, as they metabolize it very slowly and this causes intoxication.

Other harmful foods for our poultry (more or less debated) are avocado, apple seeds, citrus fruits, onion, bread, sugar and salt, rice, egg shells, raw meat and sausages.

FINAL TIPS ON PROPER FEEDING OF CHICKENS

The ideal is to feed our laying hens twice a day (before and after grazing) taking into account the fact that during the winter and during the egg-laying period they have a greater daily need for food. Indicatively, a laying hen weighing about 2 kg has a daily requirement of about 130 gr. of feed (it must be considered that the requirement grows with increasing weight). Feed should never be advanced inside the chicken coop as it could create mold and / or attract the attention of mice, pigeons or other unwelcome guests. Finally, it is absolutely important to combine a correct diet with plenty of fresh water, correctly managing the drinking trough of our chicken coop (the hens drink a lot and the addition of apple cider vinegar could be useful for example to provide potassium and sulfur and intestinal parasites).

WATER IN THE CHICKEN COOP

Hens drink a lot, more than other birds, and for this it is essential to have a suitable drinking trough that guarantees a supply of fresh water constantly available to them inside the hen house. On a hot summer day they can drink up to 17 fl oz.

The daily water requirement is proportional to the weight of the hen; in general it must be taken into account that, compared to any other domestic animal, hens have a need twice as high and approximately, in quantitative terms, a water consumption equal to 2-3 times that of the weight of the feed ingested (estimating about 5 oz per day of food, we therefore obtain about 8.5-14 fl oz. of water per day).

The optimal water temperature is between 50 ° F and 60 ° F. Drinking too cold water can cause a lowering of the body temperature of our laying hens with consequent reduction of egg laying (as well as congestion and gastroenteritis) drinking water that is too hot can lead to excessive consumption of water aimed at compensating for the overwhelming sense of thirst. During the day, the hens drink in small quantities, but very frequently.

To swallow the water, they have to tilt their heads back because they are otherwise unable to swallow. To monitor the health of our hens it is good to keep the amount of water drunk under control (also for this reason it is recommended that the drinking trough is made in such a way that it cannot be overturned). For example, excessive water consumption could also be caused by a diet that is too rich in salt and therefore, even this factor, must be absolutely monitored. If we observe abnormal water consumption for a long period (very low or too excessive) it may be necessary to consult a veterinarian.

A good natural remedy of ancient tradition (even if not ascertained and supported by studies) consists in adding a teaspoon of apple cider vinegar for every liter of water in the drinking trough (about 0.10 fl oz. For each liter).

Doing so not only reduces the formation of bacteria in the water itself, but also provides substances useful for the well-being of the hen (such as sulfur and potassium), which are essential to maintain a naturally acidic environment in the digestive tract (lower the PH of the gastrointestinal tract) and therefore able to block the development of bacteria and fungi (it has in fact been found to be an effective method against Candida, Pseudomonas and coccidiosis).

However, by exceeding the dose of vinegar, the hens may no longer like the taste of the water and therefore, by avoiding drinking it, damage can occur; therefore pay close attention to the recommended doses; in addition, there are specific products on the market, specifically designed for the consumption of hens, based on apple vinegar.

The apple cider vinegar added to the water is absorbed by the intestine in the necessary quantity while the excess part is naturally eliminated with the excretions. It is also important to point out that the use of water and apple cider vinegar does not induce any risk of altering the calcification of the egg shells.

On the contrary, water acidulated with lemon can instead hinder the absorption of calcium in the intestine and therefore make it unavailable to be metabolized into bones, egg shells (resulting in the deposition of soft-shelled eggs), muscles, nerves, etc.

Bird Feeders and Racks

For a correct feeding of our laying hens, in addition to the quality of the food, it is also very important to use the most suitable accessories as regards the feeder, both for grains and feed (feeders), and for any fresh grass or large leafy vegetables. (such as black cabbage, very welcome!). There are many types of chicken feeders on the market, even very ingenious ones, and each one suitable for solving any small problems specific to each individual hen house.

A first important feature of a feeder for grains and feed is to prevent our hens from scratching inside, dirtying the food or causing it to tip over on the ground and consequently waste. Furthermore, the feed dispersed on the ground can be a source of attraction for birds and small rodents (especially mice), and it is therefore important that it is avoided.

In our grandparents' chicken coops, the problem of overturning the manger (or even the drinking trough) was often solved with heavy stone bowls, so heavy that they could not be overturned even by the weight of a large hopping hen.

Another fact to pay attention to is the type and number of feeders to be installed in the chicken coop based on the number of hens and their hierarchical behavior; in all chicken coops the "law" of the pecking order applies, according to which the dominant specimens peck first and, only subsequently, can they peck all the others, always in strict hierarchical order.

It is therefore important to check that the specimens that will have last access to the manger still manage to find some food and not be without it. Sometimes a good method to solve this problem can be to place two feeders at such a distance from each other so that, in moving the dominants from one to the other, they are able to fit in and eat even "the most hierarchically weak hens".

It is also important that the feeders are placed in any case protected from the rain (for example under the small shed of the garden fence or, if possible, inside the shelter house); as they must remain absolutely dry.

Indicatively, for each specimen, a portion of food equal to about 4.5 oz per day should be available.

Current chicken feeders on the market have become truly reliable and in addition to avoiding this problem of dispersion of the content, they are also able to counteract other problems, such as contamination of food with feces and access to food by birds and mice.

CHICKEN FEEDER WITH BOWL

In the case of the simple bowl feeder for hens it is important that it has a slightly raised edge, that it is made with a material that is not too light (steel, terracotta or ceramic could be fine, also because it is easy to clean) and that it is positioned overhead (for example placed on a box or fixed to a wall or on a pedestal). Economic, hygienic and anti-waste solution.

HOPPER FEEDER FOR CHICKENS

If you have chosen a hopper for a chicken feeder, grains and feed are contained in a container (often fixed to the wall) from which they descend by gravity into a collection tray below. They are perhaps the oldest mangers, initially also made of wood by the expert hands of breeders.

Today, on the market, there are various types and they are certainly an excellent solution: economical, hygienic and anti-waste. They also have the advantage of guaranteeing a constant presence of grains and feed even for a fairly long period (depending on the size of the "tank").

SIPHON FEEDER

The siphon chicken feeder is usually found on the market in plastic or galvanized sheet metal (both very easy to clean). They are tanks in the shape of a truncated cone that rest on a circular containment base with the edges higher than the level of the feed that descends by gravity.

This type of feeder can either be placed on a box, on a wall support, or mounted suspended. The siphon feeder is also an economical, hygienic and anti-waste solution, and guarantees a constant presence of grains and feed for a fairly long period (depending on the size of the "tank").

To protect against nocturnal "food theft", especially by rodents, it would be advisable to place the manger in an area of the chicken coop that is closed and inaccessible or keep them suspended from the ground.

HOPPER CHICKEN FEEDER WITH PEDAL AND ANTI-LOOTING CANTILEVERED LID

The pedal feeder for hens is normally closed and opens only when the hen gets on the platform, and remains open as long as the hen eats, closing only when the animal gets off it. Initially it will be necessary to help our hens to become familiar with the mechanism, but then it will be simple and comfortable for them too.

It is a slightly cheaper solution than the mangers we have seen previously (at least if it is not made with your own hands), but it is certainly hygienic, anti-waste and is a 100% "anti-theft" solution, for this reason it is called anti-looting.

Depending on the size of the "tank", they guarantee the constant presence of grains and feed even for a fairly long period.

DIY "ORGAN PIPE" CHICKEN FEEDER

The "organ pipe" DIY chicken feeder is another practical and effective economic, hygienic and anti-waste solution, to be made on an internal wall of the chicken coop, through a simple and ingenious use of common plumbing pipes.

THE RACK

Especially in the event that our chicken coop has a small lawn area or even only temporarily "resting" (for example inside the enclosure), it is important to provide our hens with fresh grass and loose leaf vegetable waste. The ideal is to place herbs and vegetables in a rack.

It could be a simple wire mesh fixed to the fence of the chicken coop or to a wall of the shelter, from which they can peck the leaves; whether it is supported or suspended, the important thing is that it is raised off the ground.

CHAPTER THREE

Chicken Coop Life

Maintenance of the Chicken Coop

(Early Autumn)

As autumn arrives, the hens in our domestic chicken coop have obviously already noticed the changes in the environment. The hours dedicated to daytime scratching decrease, while those spent in the night shelter increase. Therefore, it is important that in the first days of autumn we proceed to a good and thorough cleaning of the chicken coop, so that it can be a healthy environment for our beloved hens, which, as we have said, will pass from now on, a lot more time inside.

Usually for the hens this is also the period of their "change of clothing", that is the natural moult, to "dress" in the plumage suitable to face the winter (during this phase, for them stressful, the animals go into productive pause).

CHICKEN COOP MAINTENANCE (OR BUILDING A NEW ONE)

The hens are very sensitive to the temperature gap between summer and autumn and in particular suffer from the air currents typical of this change of season (we can also provide them with a simple roof covered on three sides, but the important thing is that there are insidious drafts). These changes in temperature can generate stress in the animal or even real respiratory diseases (as happens to us with colds, even hens can have sneezing, nasal discharge, loss of appetite and difficulty breathing well).

We also keep in mind that the increase in environmental humidity, after the summer drought, also has the positive consequence of reinvigorating the vegetation of the pasture where our hens can go back to scratching to find important food.

For the construction of the shelter, where it does not already exist or if you want to build a new one, you have two options: either buy a new chicken coop on the market (increasingly specialized) or take the path of self-construction.

The beginning of autumn can also be the ideal time to decide to change the layout and position of our chicken coop, both to have a clean and perhaps more functional little house, and to move it to a different area of our garden-vegetable garden (the ideal would be to place the perch-shelter in the shade during the summer, and in full sun in the winter;

the proximity of deciduous plants would solve this aspect in a natural way, especially if the chicken coop is oriented towards the south).

It is also time to shelter the sand and ash bath so that it can remain as dry as possible during the rainy months of the year.

CLEANING THE CHICKEN COOP: SHELTER AND ACCESSORIES

In order to ensure the hygiene of the hen house and the health of our hens, the beginning of autumn is the optimal period (together with spring) to carry out one of the two most consistent annual cleanings.

This extraordinary cleaning is actually a real sanitization, aimed at preventing any infestation of parasites or other physical / organic problems to the hens.

During this operation, it is advisable to thoroughly sanitize the chicken coop and all equipment (nests, perches, feeders and drinking troughs) and, in cases where it is not cleaned continuously, the permanent litter should be removed.

It is recommended to thoroughly clean the shelter, preferably using a steam pressure washer (if you do not have one you can always rent it). It is possible to use natural pesticides based on essential oils or extracts of various plants; on the other hand, where it is decided to use disinfectants marketed by the main pharmaceutical and zootechnical companies (for example Chlorhexidine, which is not very toxic for hens and kills bacteria and fungi), it is necessary to respect the times of the "sanitary vacuum" (usually a couple of weeks), removing the hens in a temporary-chicken coop (in this phase no animal must enter the sanitized shelter; maximum attention also to dogs and cats).

Beyond the operation of sanitizing the chicken coop, it is absolutely essential to follow the "good practices" of daily management, that is that the covered environment is kept dry and with a well-contained litter (and, where possible, with a natural fermentation in course, which would guarantee maximum hygiene).

Among the most important precautions we believe it is useful to point out that the roost and the night shelter (below which all nocturnal manure will be concentrated and collected) should be separated as much as possible.

Sometimes, in the case of infections and diseases from parasites, it may be appropriate to use specific products available at the retailers of agricultural products, carefully looking at the instructions since they will provide very precise dilutions and dosages (and which sometimes will have to be distributed with backpack pump on all surfaces of the chicken coop to be cleaned such as walls, floor, ceiling, etc.).

During this eventuality, it would not be bad to open and ventilate the spaces, giving the sun the opportunity to directly irradiate even the usually closed parts, depending on the type of chicken coop structure.

PASTURE CARE

Among the positive aspects of early autumn there is certainly the reinvigoration of the areas intended for grazing. In fact, the higher environmental humidity favors, after the summer drought, the development of new grassy vegetation, and it is time to return to pay attention to the grassy lawn for grazing.

If possible, it would be optimal to provide green spaces to be allocated to the hens in alternating periods, in such a way as to allow a homogeneous use of the land and allow the vegetation to regenerate (the constant presence of free-range hens in fact causes its total disappearance in a short time).

In this period, the thickening and regrowth of grass can be facilitated also by throwing dry vegetation on the lawn; the soil, thanks to the heat generated by this cover and by the fermentation process of the withered plants, will ensure rapid germination of each small seed.

In the event that you have dry leaves raked around the house, it is suggested to make them available to the hens in the area of the hen house; in fact, the hens love to "rummage" in the piles of leaves in search of food.

(Winter)

In the winter months, as the hours of light decrease, the hens rest and egg production reduces or even stops. Then, as the hours of light increase (photoperiod, therefore after the winter solstice of 21 December), the hens will begin to awaken from this sort of winter "laying hibernation". However, it should be pointed out that it is not only the cold that is primarily responsible for the interruption of egg laying, but also the decrease in hours of light, and the issue is hormonal.

While some breeds of laying hens stop production for only a week, other breeds have a longer rest period, even a month or more. And it is precisely with the arrival of January that the hours of daylight return to increase and the hens in our hen house start laying eggs again.

Raising hens naturally also means accepting this natural reaction to seasonality. To overcome this "problem" and keep egg production constant even in winter, sometimes the chicken coops are artificially illuminated for a few hours, in order to achieve the necessary daily photoperiod of light; certainly it is a very different and less invasive practice than keeping the hens 24 hours under the neon lights as happens in large industrial poultry farms. In my opinion it is always a human action that interferes with the animal's biological clock and for self-consumption we believe it is possible to give up our eggs for a few days.

FEEDING THE HENS DURING THE WINTER

A possible concrete help to stimulate egg production even in winter could consist in supporting our hens with a more energetic diet, which stimulates the increase of body fat, increasing portions and preferring, for example, the use of protein and fat feed or even the use of oil seeds and even oats.

Furthermore, during the winter, given the lack of green pasture, it may be good practice to increase the supply of vegetables (for example, cabbage leaves, of which they are very greedy!), In order to make up for the possible lack of some vitamins and mineral salts. Another idea may be to add dried nettle or hemp seeds to the grains. In general, however, adding a little seasonal fruit and vegetables is certainly an excellent choice, also to prepare the animals for the next breeding season, when they need to be in top shape.

IMPORTANT PRECAUTIONS

Especially in areas where winter is really harsh, there are some precautions that need to be taken to help our hens get through the winter, which will make them "happy hens" even in the cold of the season.

PAY ATTENTION TO THE RISK OF DISEASE

The month of January is one of the coldest and most humid months and for the hens in our chicken coop it is a period in which they are put to the test also in terms of resistance to diseases. In this month (as well as in the particularly cold and humid months) it is important that the shelter and the area of the fence (or garden) is kept particularly clean (increasing the number of hours at night consequently increases the number of hours spent inside the house and on the perches, and therefore the quantity of manure produced increases; furthermore, the "permanent litter" in the garden fence and in the paved spaces of the chicken coops must always be well drained and dry): it is therefore essential to take care of the hygiene of the chicken coop for the health of our hens.

It will therefore be essential to keep our hens under daily control, looking for any signs of disease in progress, in order to intervene immediately in the treatment, preventing the situation from worsening and putting the animal at vital risk.

With the bitter cold, the hens will most likely tend to move and scratch less than usual and for this it may be necessary to induce them to move, for example by placing water, vegetable racks and feed in the feeders in distant points from each other, in such a way as to push them to walk from one point to another.

ENSURE THE AVAILABILITY OF WATER

It is very important to pay attention to the availability of water in the drinking trough; in this month (and more generally in winter) it could easily freeze and it is therefore important to check it often, so that the hens always have liquid water available (remember that they have a great need to drink, even if in smaller quantities compared to spring and summer).

In case of availability of electricity at the chicken coop, in extremely harsh weather conditions it might be worth considering using heated bowls (usually used for dogs and cats, but easily adaptable to our chicken coop).

AVOID FREEZING OF LEGS, CRESTS AND WATTLES

In the case of heavy snowfall, it will be important to create a space or a "split" path free from it, in order to avoid freezing of the legs that could occur if the hens were forced to move outdoors in the snow for hours.

Another idea to help our animals could be to insert some overhead "objects" in the pasture such as pallets, stumps and large branches that are raised from the ground and higher than the snow, in order to act as a non-frozen "refuge" to give relief to the paws.

In addition, in the case of temperatures below 32° F, it will be important to counter the freezing of ridges and wattles by using petroleum jelly or olive oil to be applied to areas sensitive to cold; Vaseline and oil can be spread at night, after the hens have gone to sleep, when they are more docile and calm. Keep in mind that for breeds with thicker crests and wattles the risk of freezing is obviously greater (and therefore even more in the rooster, again due to the larger size).

SAFEGUARD THE EGGS FROM FREEZING AND BREAKING

If the cold conditions are really extreme, it will be important to immediately collect the eggs in the nest so that they do not freeze and risk breaking (the eggs are composed of about 75% of water!).

Our advice is to gradually acclimate the hens to the colder climate by closing any openings and drafts in the henhouse, as well as creating additional shelter barriers around it (also taking into account the possible weight of the snow on the roof of the shed, evaluating well the "load capacity").

If you think that your shelter is not sufficiently insulated, you could easily intervene manually and do-it-yourself by inserting a thickness/padding made with straw, necessarily clean and dry.

Another aspect of the chicken coop to be evaluated in winter and which is often overlooked is the height. Hot air, as is well known, tends to rise upwards, so a chicken coop with a very high ceiling will disperse much more heat than one with a low roof, which instead favors more stagnation of hot air at "hen height".

So, if you have a very high chicken coop you could consider intervening in time by lowering the ceiling "artificially" with plywood boards; it can be removed once the cold season has passed.

The hens will then tend to perch and fall asleep closer to each other, to keep each other warm, and therefore even the only intervention of greater containment of their heat inside the hen house can be very important (taking into account that each hen is able to develop the equivalent of 10 Watts of heat, it will be important to adopt thermal insulation solutions to avoid the dispersion of this natural heat).

But be careful: reducing air currents and improving thermal insulation does not mean eliminating ventilation from the chicken coop; it will be essential to leave a good internal air circulation to guarantee the health of the hens (excellent in this sense is the vasistas window opening that directs the cold area upwards, mixing it with the hot one without directly hitting the animals). An excess of ammonia formation and stagnation in the night shelter environment can cause various very serious disorders (from visual and respiratory complications to even skin burns). Always remember that the hens that are acclimatized to sleep outdoors even in the winter months will be healthy and robust free-range hens (it is important to pay attention to the choice of poultry breeds as local as possible or in any case suitable for the specific microclimate).

If we assume the use of an electric heater to heat the environment, it is first necessary to examine the safety conditions and the guarantees of stability.

The safety conditions are to be evaluated in terms of fire risk (wood, shavings, straw or other materials inside the hen house are easily flammable).

The guarantees of stability are equally important because in the event of a blackout there could be a sudden drop in the temperature in the hen house which could cause a thermal shock to which our hens would not be able to react, especially if the absence of light occurs at deep night.

BUT WHAT ARE THE MOST SUITABLE BREEDS OF CHICKENS FOR COLD CLIMATES?

In general, all rustic breeds (such as Polverara, Leghorn, Hamburg, etc.) resist quite well even to cold temperatures, obviously putting into practice all the precautions and attentions discussed so far.

Another remarkably robust breed is the Italian Barrata (local name of the barred Plymouth Rock) which in 1938 was successfully subjected to a breeding experiment in the Alta Val di Susa at an altitude of 6118 feet above sea level.

Finally, if you want to be really calm, you can take breeds suitable for living in very extreme latitudes, such as the Chantecler (breed created specifically to withstand the cold climate of Canada), the Dominican (a breed that well tolerates North America cold winters), or the Siberian Calzata (progenitor of many current Russian breeds).

How to Introduce New Chickens in an Existing Chicken Coop

Introducing new chickens to your flock is something most chicken keepers have to figure out at some point.

When we tried introducing new chickens to our existing flock for the first time we made one huge mistake and learned the hard way what to do and what not to do.

Here's the thing:

Chickens are really serious about their pecking order. When introducing new chickens to your flock, older chickens will terrorize younger ones and can do significant damage if not introduced properly. Whether you have a small backyard flock or a larger brood of chickens, in this post I'll tell you how to introduce new chickens or pullets so that it goes as smoothly as possible.

WHAT IS THE PECKING ORDER?

Chickens are social animals (just like humans). They have an order to their social hierarchy that is determined by pecking, hence the "pecking order". Bigger, stronger, more aggressive chickens basically bully their way to the top, while smaller less aggressive (I'd even say pacifist) chickens are lower on the hierarchy. If there is a rooster, he will be at the top of the pecking order. If not, a dominate hen will take that spot.

The pecking order is one reason that you don't want to have a bunch of roosters in your flock. They may (will) kill each other for the top spot. You shouldn't have more than 1 rooster for every 12-15 hens.

If the decision is made, and new chickens have to be added to our chicken coop, it is good, first of all, to know that this action, at least at first, will destabilize a little "the environment" and the harmony of the group " was created.

This is absolutely normal and there is no need to be alarmed by some pecks, runs, cackles or ruffles.

THE NEW CHICKENS COULD BE CARRIERS OF DISEASES OR PARASITES

It could be possible that the new hens we want to put in our chicken coop are carriers of diseases or parasites that we know nothing about.

Mixing them immediately with the others could be a rash and risky action and therefore we strongly recommend a quarantine period, isolated from the others, after which, if everything is alright, we can be sure that they are healthy animals.

In this period of quarantine, we will have to pay close attention to nutrition, perhaps including some foods in the diet such as apple cider vinegar in water and minced garlic in food, which help to contain some of the most common parasites.

Even the chicken coop litter could be contaminated with pathogens capable of attacking the new hens, therefore, once the quarantine has been passed and time to insert the latest arrivals has come, it would be advisable to first clean the chicken coop and spread a new litter box of mixed straw and wood shavings.

TIMING

it is always good to insert the new chickens during the night, when the "old tenants" (and the new ones) are sleeping. This allows for a much softer and less stressful transition for everyone.

Important warning: if there are many chickens living in your chicken coop, never introduce a single new one. The unfortunate will be the target of all the others and will undergo a really heavy and stressful treatment. So try to insert more new specimens together, so that they in turn create a small group able to better counter the attacks of the other group, and to defend each other.

It could be a good thing to set up physical "shelters" (stone barriers, boards, bushes, perches, etc.) in the enclosure and in the area around the chicken coop. Bullied hens can find shelter and a bit of calm behind or above them.

If we find that the entry of the new chicken in the hen house produces too many attacks and stress, one thing to do may be to divide the space with a network with wide links, so that the two groups begin to know each other and "smell" each other without coming into physical contact and then, after a couple of weeks spent like this, try to put them all back together. In 99% of cases this technique always solves the problem.

MISSION ACCOMPLISHED?

Usually, after about a couple of weeks, the new chickens entering the hen house should have been accepted by the others and have found their place within the new hierarchy of the group.

During the period of "instability" it is always good practice to check the animals every day to be sure that there are no injuries, which could worsen over the days. If we find a wounded animal it is good to put it aside, treat it and only when it is perfectly healthy again, reintroduce it into the hen house (so as not to trigger any feather pecking stimulated by the sight of blood).

Another thing to do, in the first days post-insertion, could be to keep the new hens closed inside the chicken coop until the afternoon, so that they learn as soon as possible where to lay their eggs, avoiding doing it in some bushes.

Does all this also apply to chicks?

Usually, when a hen is hatching (so we are talking about natural hatching, or artificial hatching in an egg incubator) it is moved (always at night) to a safe and quiet place, far from the others.

Once the chicks are born, the mother hen can stay with them for about 1 to 2 months, but if she starts laying eggs and eating on her own first, then it is best to put her back in the hen house early, because she could peck her own chicks.

However, the chicks must be kept separate from the rest of the animals until the age of about 3 months. To facilitate the return to the group, they can be placed in an area separated from the others with a network, so that in any case the process of insertion and habit begins even in the absence of direct physical contact. At this point, during the night, they can then be placed in the chicken coop.

WHAT IF I HAVE TO INSERT A NEW ROOSTER?

Roosters, as it is known, are much more combative and bloodthirsty than hens, and therefore it is absolutely not recommended to insert an adult rooster inside a chicken coop where another rooster is already present: the two could collide very violently and bring back deep wounds, even fatal.

If you really have to insert a new rooster, do it when it is still small, so that the present dominant does not perceive it as a direct competitor. This will certainly not avoid some skirmishes over time, but everything should remain within a few pecks at most.

Finally, it is always good to remember that for each rooster there should never be less than 5/8 hens available in the ratio (the ratio between rooster and hens depends on the breed; in the case of heavy breeds, 4/5 females for each male, while for the light rustics it takes about 8/10).

AGGRESSIVE ROOSTER

In order to prevent or reduce the aggression of roosters (especially where their behavior leads to dangerous attacks), it is possible to try putting some approaches into practice, which could also be decisive (at least in some cases); the measures described below are the result of empirical evidence and common sense assessments that can be tried without any contraindication, neither for the rooster nor for us.

The ultimate purpose of these methodologies is to be able to make the rooster perceive us as superior to him in the hierarchical scale, making sure that this gives us the opportunity to find a balance point in terms of mutual respect.

However, a first necessary recommendation regarding children should be made: children should always be kept at a distance from aggressive roosters, unless an adult is there with them to monitor the situation (children cannot have total awareness of how they they must behave in front of an aggressive animal such as a rooster which, in relation to a "human cub", can be very dangerous).

To try to stem and correct the excessive aggression of a rooster, we must first understand its origin.

In nature, a rooster's primary task is to defend its own group of hens from possible rivals (other roosters) in search of females to mate with (which means continuation of the species according to the genetic line of the strongest).

Precisely for this reason, a rooster's aggression will most likely increase during the spring-summer, or in the most favorable period for mating and reproduction.

An aggressive rooster can lash out at a person (adult or child) after chasing him and attacking with pecks, claws and ramming. And he won't stop chasing us until, according to him, we no longer pose a threat to his chickens.

Before the rooster decides to launch its attack, we can usually recognize some characteristic "warning" movements that can help us defend ourselves; among the most blatant actions are the lowering of the head while staring at us and a slight sway of the body. If we notice them, ready to drive it back.

Solutions

Since they are chicks, we can try to get them used to our presence and contact as much as possible, taking them in hand and in arms, especially inside the hen house and in front of the hens. It is advisable to talk to him in calm tones and try to feed him from your hand and then put him back on the ground when he is calm. This relationship of closeness and trust can help when it is necessary to play a dominant role to define the rules of mutual respect.

Even if a rooster brings us "gifts" (pebbles, twigs, seeds, kernels, worms or other) it is important to clarify that it does not do it for an unconditional act of love, but because in this way it wants prove that he is the "boss" and we are one of his "subordinate chickens".

At about 4/5 months of age, the hormones will begin to increase the tendency to aggression in the rooster. In a few weeks our little chick will have grown into a testosterone-filled young rooster and will need to defend its territory and its "flock" by chasing away intruders and possible suitors, including those who raised them!

having raised a rooster from a chick is an excellent starting point for being able to control its aggression in the future, but it is by no means a guarantee.

On the other hand, teaching behavioral rules to an aggressive rooster received or acquired during its reproductive age is truly a very complicated and difficult challenge to win.

How to manage and reduce the aggression of your rooster

Among the most sensible tips to manage and reduce a rooster's aggression we can list the following:

1. let's move slowly inside the chicken coop, without making sudden movements. For roosters (as well as for all animals) every movement has a meaning and incorrect or rash movements could be an unforgivable communication error. A sudden movement could amount, in the rooster mind, to a danger or an attack.

2. our rooster needs to learn that "he is not our leader" but that "we are the leader", and that we will not in any way hinder his life purpose, which can be summarized in the protection of his hens and mating.

Our presence must be perceived as a sort of position as an alpha outsider (super partes). To this end, we will not have to tolerate and let go of any small challenge to our "dominant" position; this means that we will have to be careful to perceive any sign of challenge and not to be taken by surprise.

3. we are asking a rooster to carry out a very demanding task, that is to change its innate and natural character and behavior. We must

therefore proceed with respect for his ethology and the work to be done to teach him that entering his space does not mean attacking him.

4. If necessary, we could use some recognizable object as a deterrent (for example a tree branch) in order to remove it or dissuade it from attacking (and not to hit it).

5. give him clear and simple signals, otherwise, we could be interpreted ambiguously and the rooster could mean that there is an attack in progress in a situation where no attack is expected.

6. Let us remember that every person who approaches the chicken coop and the rooster will have to follow our instructions and be careful not to "launch involuntary challenges" (for this reason it is very important not to leave children alone with an aggressive rooster).

A further possible attempt is to approach the rooster during its night sleep; even in this case, keep in mind that you will be perceived by the animal as a threat, therefore, you will have to make yourself recognized as friends, with extreme delicacy.

Pay attention to your every movement and to every movement of the rooster; maybe wrap it in a blanket to avoid getting scratched if it suddenly wriggles out.

By repeating all these tricks over time it is possible to try to reduce the aggressive behavior of your rooster.

Behavior training program

After having tested all the aforementioned measures, which require a certain consistency and constancy of our behavior towards the rooster, we could evaluate the opportunity to proceed with a sort of real exercise (for us and for our rooster) aimed at affirming " who's the Boss".

The success of the exercise consists in launching a challenge and "winning it in theory" without there being any combat, thus succeeding in affirming our "hierarchical superiority".

Our goal is not to be mean and disrespectful, but to be able to get our rooster to respect us.

We need to get him to respect our position as an alpha member and this will make his attacks much less likely.

During all interactions with our rooster it is important to remain calm, calm and assertive. The consistency of all our interactions is certainly the most important element.

You can decide to wear protective clothing: long boots, long pants, a long-sleeved shirt and any protective goggles are recommended.

The challenge consists in affirming our dominant position by entering the "living space" of our rooster, that proximity beyond which we know that we run the risk of alarming it and producing an attack (it is a space that is not measured in meters and that varies from rooster to rooster).

Once we have identified the space, we take a big decisive step inside it, fixing the rooster firmly while keeping our head tilted down (possibly even keeping our hands on the hips simulating the movement of spreading the wings).

The rooster should start fidgeting, looking away (turning his head), standing still and looking down (sometimes pretending to find and peck something on the ground).

If we manage to get the rooster away this means that we have won the "virtual challenge" and at this point it is important that we move firmly away from space.

It is in fact a real challenge for us too, who rightly and undeniably will have a certain fear of being attacked during this exercise (it is therefore important to be on guard).

It is essential to do this exercise without fear (and this is really difficult for many people); fear is perceived as a weakness in the animal kingdom and it is the perception of this weakness that could incite our rooster to attack us.

But even if we are a little afraid, the important thing is to be able to not make any movement that could amount to an attempt to move away: we must be able to get him to be the first to move backwards.

If instead of retreating, while we remain motionless, it begins to move towards us, we remain as still as possible, and continue to firmly guard our position (a similar attitude is recommended, for example, even when we are attacked in a way close by a dog).

If it raises its wings and slightly expands them ready for attack, we do the same. We spread our arms, continue to stare directly at him, and step back into his space towards him. It most likely will fall back.

At this point it was stated who is the boss. We will have to continue to move slowly and respectfully, without further attacking our rooster, who has just suffered a defeat.

It is not certain that this exercise will be successful on the first attempt or that it is sufficient to do it once; you may also realize it is not a viable path with your rooster, or that it is a useful tool to practice consistently and that will give good or excellent results over time.

Obviously each case must be evaluated individually and this is not an applicable "recipe" for all cases.

Conclusion

Always remember to look at everything in the right perspective, reminding us that the natural behavior of roosters is not quiet and meek like that of a hen; our "being leaders" and our supremacy should not be harsh or violent, but we will be excellent breeders if we manage to be respected by being recognized as a "gentle authority".

Once we have found the right balance, we will also be able to aspire to establish a level of trust that will allow us to peck something from the hand and perhaps be able to pick up even our most "difficult" rooster.

FEATHER PECKING

Chickens will always peck at each other a little bit, this is almost an essential part of establishing a "pecking order" or hierarchy amongst the flock. So the 'top hen' will peck at others and the lowest bird in the order will be pecked most.

Most of the time this isn't a real problem and you'll probably find that the bird at the bottom of the social order will merely high tail it away if it gets fed up and no real damage is done. However, if your hens are kept in an enclosed run, simply running away might not be an option.

Feather pecking is, as the name suggests, when one hen starts pecking at another's feathers and pulls them out causing distress to the birds and, in some cases, draws blood from a wound.

This is not to be confused with an over-amorous cockerel who can often pull feathers out of a hens back while trying to gain a perch, or even the annual moult. Feather pecking often occurs around the hen's vent, tail or head. A good indication that feather pecking is occurring is not only bald patches on the birds but the sign of half eaten feathers around the coop.

Chickens are attracted to the color red (one reason why so many poultry feeders and drinkers are red) so the comb, wattle and the vent - which is often reddened after laying an egg - draws the attention of other hens. Chickens are also attracted to blood, the color and smell (they are after all essentially mini dinosaurs) so, if wounds are left untreated, it will only attract them more. Always make sure you treat any blood or wounds straight away with either a gentian violet spray or a wound powder, for the well-being of the bird.

Stress is also one of the top reasons for feather pecking. A chicken coop that is too hot will stress the birds, try to increase the ventilation to cure this problem. If you have too many hens in one hen house or poultry run, the lack of space will stress them. Can you reduce the overcrowding? As a guide a hen should be allowed 1 to 2 sq ft in their house with 7 "-8" of perch space to roost.

When laying an egg especially, chickens like the area to be dim and quiet, excessive or glaring lights will only stress them and reduce egg laying. A chicken coop should have at least one nest space for 4 to 5 birds.

Anti-Feather Pecking Sprays can help to break a feather pecking habit such as this. The spray is applied to the victim bird, it creates a foul taste in the perpetrators mouth, helping to deter them from pecking. Some pecking sprays are clear liquids and contain antiseptics, whilst others are brown and based on Stockholm Tar which is an old traditional method to stop pecking or biting. You may find one type will work with your flock whilst another may not so you may need some trial and error to find the right one.

It is sprayed all around the wound area. When the chicken that's been doing the pecking gets a mouthful of that, then they will stop pecking and pulling out feathers.

PICA AND CANNIBALISM

Where does this "perverse" deviation of behavior originate? Among the main causes there is certainly the lack of space and the consequent overcrowding of the chicken coop, insufficiency of feeders and drinking troughs, and in general animals in high stress.

It is a serious phenomenon, which should not be underestimated, as by imitation, it can easily spread and involve many specimens.

The specimens attacked by this "mania", peck each other furiously, especially on the head, neck, back and the area around the cloaca, until they get bleeding wounds that stimulate this behavior even more. And even if initially it may seem limited to a few subjects, in a very short time it can spread by imitation, up to involving them all.

The stress that then triggers feather pecking and cannibalism usually derives from a life spent in too narrow and overcrowded spaces (this is why it is a well-known phenomenon in large industrial farms), with an insufficient number of feeders and drinking troughs which increases the level of competitiveness for food, and therefore the stress of the animal.

Thus, at a certain point, the first signs of feather pecking begin, which then, at the sight of the blood, degenerate into real cannibalism.

Animals attacked by this ailment are reduced in a pitiful way, with patches of bare skin and bleeding wounds which, moreover, if not properly treated, can give rise to infections and other diseases.

How to prevent feather pica and cannibalism in hens

1. First of all, our hens need lots of outdoor space, where they can roam freely during the day

2. check the state of the hens and verify that they are not injured, if so, they must be isolated immediately.

3. Spread the food in several places to avoid crowding and fighting over food.

4. Try to keep the hens "busy" as much as possible for example by hanging vegetable leaves at a certain height. It is also possible to provide them with games, rides and swings to keep them busy.

Obviously, the sand and ash bath should not be missing, which for hens is an area of relaxation as well as providing them with protection from parasites.

5. Pay attention to the food given, in fact scraps of raw meat and cured meats can transmit diseases or even increase the aggressiveness of chickens.

6. Do not expose animals to artificial light during the evening or night, which greatly increases their stress. Poultry have a circadian wake-sleep rhythm which is the natural day-night rhythm, with hormonal and health processes influenced by sunlight.

7. Raising chickens near sources of excessive noise can also cause them great stress.

8. Make sure there is neither too much light nor too hot in the shelter, and that the perches are large enough to comfortably accommodate all the hens. Furthermore, the litter box must always be in excellent condition, and must not release a bad smell of ammonia into the environment.

9. Make sure that the chickens are not suffering from a parasite attack that weakens and stresses them (eg lice, pollen and mites).

If you learn how to manage hens and chicken coops correctly, no cases of feather pecking or cannibalism should arise.

but anything can happen, and if the problem does arise, there are practices that can be adopted to resolve the situation.

The first solution, even if feasible in extreme cases, is the cutting of the beak. Even if the solution is the least desirable, it could save many animals. However, cutting the beak is a special intervention that can be painful and very stressful for the hen, which, if on the one hand it no longer hurts its fellowmen, on the other hand it does not allow it to live its life naturally (pecking food, etc.).

Another practice is to buy and use special "glasses" for hens.

Our chicken can start eating materials which are not fit for consumption, such as feathers, litter material, threads, etc. although it is less commonly found in modern poultry farm, it may come from parasitic infestation, new litter material and Phosphorus deficiency. I think the latter is the main reason for developing pica, beyond this other vitamin and mineral deficiencies also play as predisposing factors. Adequate vitamins, amino acids, minerals addition, changing the litter, space extension and adding enzymes could reduce the problem.

How to Deal with Chicken Diseases

Part of raising chickens is understanding how to recognize and treat some of their common illnesses.

No matter what you use your chickens for, keeping your birds happy and healthy is always a priority in raising them. Most tend to be easy keepers, but occasionally (just as we all do) when they get sick or are having issues, we must deal with it. Here are some of the most common health problems you might face with your flock.

Fortunately, for the average poultryman, good management, the ability to detect disease or parasite problems at an early stage, and the knowledge and judgment to know when and where to go for help when needed should make it possible for him or her to cope successfully with most disease and parasite problems. In this chapter an attempt will be made to present the causes of disease and the basic concepts of disease prevention and control along with examples of the most serious and prevalent poultry diseases.

Behavioral Diseases

If your birds are acting aggressive, pecking other birds, or excessively plucking feathers, (as we saw in the previous chapter) this could be a sign of a behavioral health problem. Stressed birds may begin eating eggs or revert to cannibalism under certain living conditions. To stop issues before they start, ensure your group has sufficient nourishment, isn't overheating or congestion. Stay aware of other general wellbeing concerns, as well.

Infectious Diseases

Poultry illnesses can be viral, bacterial, or contagious and will and they will easily spread from bird to bird. These diseases can influence your chickens organs like intestine, nerves, lungs, reproductive or immune system, just as their skin. In the unlikely case (but not too much) that any of your chicken give indications of a poultry sickness, it's critical to separate the ill chicken from the others, as to protect your hens.

One method of classification is to consider the system the organism affects. Examples of respiratory bacterial diseases include colibacillosis, infectious coryza, and fowl cholera infections. Examples of bacterial infections affecting internal organs are paratyphoid, pullorum, fowl typhoid, and omphalitis.

Colibacillosis

This is characterized by anyone of a group of infectious diseases in which E. coli is the primary or secondary causative agent. E. coli is part of the natural gut flora and is an opportunistic pathogen that can become a problem when stress or disease occurs. All birds are carriers. Diagnosis is through laboratory isolation of the coliform organism.

Many antibiotics and drugs are used for treatment but preventive management such as good sanitation and minimizing

stress are still the best procedures.

Infectious coryza is a respiratory disease caused by Haemophilus gallinarum, a gram-negative nonmotile bacteria. The disease is characterized by nasal discharge, swelling of the face, and sneezing. Lesions include inflamed nasal passages and sinuses with discharges of yellow mucus and cheesy exudates in the cavities. Treatments are numerous and vaccination is available. All-in, all-out rearing and keeping young bird flocks away from older flocks is one control method.

Fowl Cholera

This illness was observed as early as 1736. The organism infects all species of poultry worldwide and is becoming an increasing problem. Birds approaching maturity or adults are most often affected. The organism is very susceptible to common disinfectants.

Transmission is by other poultry, wild birds, predators, and rodents. Infection can occur through the respiratory tract, eyes, or open wounds. One characteristic feature of fowl cholera is that it occurs rapidly. Birds will be found dead with no explanation. As the disease progresses, birds lose weight, decrease feed and increase water consumption, have pale yellow droppings, and sometimes produce a rattling noise from mucus in their air passages. A differential diagnosis is necessary because symptoms can be similar to other respiratory diseases. Positive identification is made by the presence of bipolar staining organisms in the blood and isolation of the causative agent. Flocks can be immunized with a three-strain cholera killed bacterin or a live "Cu" vaccine. Treatment products include sulfadimethoxine, sulfaquinoxaline, and oxytetracycline.

Fowl Pox

This highly contagious viral infection comes in two forms, dry and wet. Dry is the most common type and is a viral infection.

In the dry form, unfeathered areas of your bird will have wart-like lesions that heal in about two weeks. The wet form of the disease features lesions appearing around the mouth and discharge from your bird's eyes.

A vaccine is available in areas where the disease is common or an outbreak occurs. Make sure to quarantine them and also, control mosquitos in your chicken enclosures since they're able to transmit the disease from flock to flock.

Marek's Disease

This is the most common yet contagious disease because it affects birds intensely: it is fatal and still untreated. Usually, it affects the younger chickens because of their weak immune systems.

If your chick has developed tumors, has irregularly shaped pupils (typically results in blindness), or develops partial paralysis, it's likely that they have Marek's Disease.

Use good sanitation practices and keep the chicks away from the adults until 5 months of age.

Infectious Bronchitis

This disease hits close to home because it wiped out half of our flock when we were new to raising chickens. You'll recognize this disease when you begin to hear your chickens sneezing, snoring, and coughing. And then the drainage will begin to secrete from their nose and eyes.

There's not much that can be done for bronchitis. You can give your birds antibiotics for a few days to make sure no other infections happen while they're sick. You can give your chickens a warm, dry place to recoup. I gave my birds a warm herb tea and fed them fresh herbs, which seemed to help.

Whether you're raising a large flock of chickens, or only a few, the process can be extremely rewarding.

However always be careful as there are many less common illnesses too. Just be sure to always pay attention to your flock and stay alert to any changes. It is better to overreact than to underreact and miss something that could be detrimental to your whole flock.

Chicken Molting

Losing feathers and re-growing them is called molting and occurs every year when the days get shorter. Molting is a normal and natural process that all hens and roosters usually carry out in early autumn (with the only exception of the Phoenix Onagadori breed male, an ancient ornamental breed from Japan, characterized by the continuous growth of the tail feathers up to to the incredible length of over 8 meters), and is a way to get a new coat after the high summer temperatures and prepare for the low temperatures of winter.

During this period, which usually lasts two months (but which can reach a maximum of 5 months), the hens stop laying eggs as they will exhaust all their energy. For this reason, to help our animals, it would be optimal to provide them with a more protein diet.

Be careful to give enough food. For example, you can buy chicks feed, which is extremely protein, and mix it with the specific feed for laying hens. This high-protein feed mix is suspended when the tail and wing feathers have regrown, a sign that the moult is coming to an end.

Do not add any more stress to the chickens than what they are already experiencing with the moult. In this period, in fact, do not introduce new chickens in the hen house, let them free to scratch on a beautiful lawn for as long as possible and away from predators and other disturbing animals, as they will not be able to fly as before and make the night shelter clean and soft.

When molting is finished, the feathers will be soft and shiny, and the eggs will usually be bigger.

If the molting lasts too short, only twenty days, it could indicate some kind of anomaly in chicken. Usually it is a lack of water, a sudden change in power supply, or a change in temperature.
Never shorten their wing feathers during this period: bleeding, physical weakness, stress and pain could in fact happen to our animal.

The Rooster

The rooster, known since ancient times as a figure and symbol of power and domination, is the true and undisputed head of the henhouse.

He is often aggressive and always tends to remember his power over other hens and other possible cocks.

The aggressiveness varies depending on the breed but another specimen of rooster around, will surely lead to a bloody fight in which one of the two will succumb.

Its aggressiveness comes from its innate will of protection of the females and of its possible progeny, present also in places where it lives in total freedom.

It is important to make it understand who's in charge, since he has no right to attack us. As we said before, you have to be careful of children, because the rooster could attack them without warning. Usually, when it senses the danger, lowers the head staring at the enemy, makes the body sway and starts the attack.

In order to reduce its aggressiveness, it would be good to go often in the henhouse moving calmly without making sudden movements, which would be badly interpreted by the animal. We can repeat the action more and more often and eventually it should get used to our presence. If necessary, you should wield a stick or something similar to avoid being attacked.

Also the fact of growing more specimens together could be a positive thing, in fact the hierarchical order will have already been established.

However, this is not synonymous with effectiveness and peace within the henhouse could be compromised.

Cock's Crow

The roosters are known for their particular "cock-a-doodle-doo". Several are the explanations of this cry in this animal: in fact, it seems to resonate its voice as a warning to other possible rivals, to attract the females, and as a general alert for every possible "stranger".

As it is customary to think, the rooster does not emit its famous call only in the morning. In fact, a team of Japanese researchers has discovered that its emission of sounds is not linked to the characteristics of the environment, but to the innate biological clock of the animal. In the experiment conducted, the researchers exposed the birds to artificial light day and night, so that they no longer distinguish daylight hours from night hours.

They, curiously, began to emit their call before the sun rose.

The rooster emits its sound mainly in places where it feels safe, where it does not perceive dangers, where its food needs are satisfied, in addition to not living in the company of other roosters who might rival him for supremacy.

Chicken Coop Management and Protection

The rooster can effectively carry out its protective task up to a maximum of fifteen hens but it is better to keep the number less than ten.

Among its main activities are the courtship of the females. In fact, it is not monogamous and innately, it tries to mate with as many females as possible.

One of the most famous courtship tactics is definitely tidbitting: when he finds a tasty morsel of food, he does a little dance and song called "tidbitting" to let the hens know about his discovery. He will let them eat first. What a gentlemen.

It is not recommended to breed very different kind of rooster, as the smaller breed would certainly suffer from this. It is easier to live with a dominant rooster with a young rooster, as the latter would likely not be perceived as a major threat.

Chickens Mating

The hens in the hen house belong to the dominant male and none are released from their seed. Only the strongest subjects will be able to reproduce and, if there are other roosters inside the henhouse, all will try to get the role of dominant rooster, starting fierce fights, especially if the submissive rooster tries to fertilize the hens.

There are two types of mating in the hens: the individual, and the group one, in which more roosters will fertilize more hens at the same time.

The hen rearing system is called a cloaca, like the male one. It is a hole where the semen of the rooster passes and then reaches the true reproductive system, the ovary. Once the fertilized egg has reached maturity, it detaches and begins a journey inside the oviduct.

It takes about 24-48 hours for the egg to be fertilized. An adult hen lays up to 5 eggs per week.

Usually, the eggs we collect in the hen house are not the result of mating. Those fertilized, in fact, will contain the chick, unlike the others. To differentiate the eggs from each other, we can put the eggs against the light, verifying the presence of a dark point with some branches, this will make us understand that it is an embryo. If, on the other hand, no stain is seen, it probably has not been fertilized.

The Chick

Taking care of the chicks is very important: they are fragile and need special care and adequate nutrition. They are born from the hen about twenty-one days of hatching.

If they are born inside an incubator, in the first 48 hours of life, they must not be taken out of the machine, nor the incubator must be opened. Similarly, if the chick was born naturally, the hen will take care of him, only make sure that the hen eats and drinks.

The chick will be ready to eat alone already after two days. If he was born inside an incubator, he would have to be placed inside a larger housing, covered with a suitable litter for feces. It is also necessary to insert a bowl of water and another bowl for the food suitable for him. Be careful when feeding chicks, in fact, it should not be the one for adults but a suitable food for its optimal growth.

Conclusion

Keeping a few chickens in a chicken coop in the garden is an activity that needs little time and can give enormous satisfaction.

The life in the hen house is almost automatic, since the hens have a very habitual life.

The chick will stay with the mother-hen for at least a month, after which it will be the hen to keep away its offsprings and to chase them away from her. At this moment you can separate the hens from the chicks and bring it back within its space in the henhouse.

COOL FACTS

Intelligence

We usually use the word "bird-brained" to refer to someone we think did something stupid, but recent research shows that chicken are, on average, more gifted than their own.

First of all, they are excellent observers as well as being able to see the world in color, better than we humans do. They enjoy an extraordinary memory that makes them able to recognize more than a hundred faces, animals or humans.

Dreaming

The hens have the ability to make real dreams as well as to enter the REM phase ("Rapid movement of the eyes"), sleep phase, connected to dreams.

Playing

Chickens like to play and make new discoveries. On the market, in fact, you can find many gadgets and real toys that will keep busy your cute garden animals.

The KFC Chicken Conspiracy

The government is said to have forced the famous fast food chain Kentucky Fried Chicken to change its name to KFC after discovering that the food sold did not come from real chickens. In fact, the hens had been so genetically modified that they no longer looked like real chickens. Fortunately a false and creepy story. In fact, KFC simply wanted to diversify its menu and use a fresher and more modern word.

Chicken Gun

When a bird collides with an airplane, it can cause considerable damage, as the speed can be really high. Scientists then created a "chicken gun" to test the safety level of aircraft by shooting chicken carcasses on stationary aircraft at a certain speed.

Hypnosis

Chicken can actually end up in a full-fledged catatonic state triggered by fear. He freezes for fear that his life will soon end. Hypnosis can also be induced in the animal, in fact, by drawing a line with chalk on the ground, placing the hen's beak on it, she will remain staring at the line and will not move unless force is used.

Finally, putting its head under the wing, chicken will think it is night and it will fall asleep.

Chickens come from dinosaurs!

The chickens, in fact, have very similar characteristics to its prehistoric ancestors such as hollow bones, the shape of the pelvis, etc. After the famous meteorite fell in the Gulf of Mexico millions of years ago, which brought about the end of most of the species living on the planet, the survivors gave birth to all living species, including today's birds.

So, which came first, the chicken or the egg?

It is up to you to find the answer to this ancient and famous enigma.

CPSIA information can be obtained
at www.ICGtesting.com
Printed in the USA
BVHW071922130421
604819BV00008BA/923